The Fritz Kreisler Collection

Original Compositions /
Transcriptions / Cadenzas
for Violin and Piano

Printed from the original editions

Compilation and Introductory Notes by Eric Wen
Foreword by Yehudi Menuhin

CARL FISCHER®
65 Bleecker Street, New York, NY 10012

ISBN 0-8258-0407-8

Table of Contents

Foreword

I am honoured and touched to be given this opportunity of paying tribute to a great violinist, musician and composer whom I loved, knew and respected and whose many works I played extensively all my life.

As a boy when I listened to Fritz Kreisler on record or during his repeated visits to San Francisco during the twenties his style opened a magic world of grace, elegance and sophistication — the world of a central Europe I had not yet encountered — which spoke so exquisitely and naturally of the beauties of society which still lay years and oceans away from an eight-year-old boy reveling in a musical repertoire from Bazzini to Mendelssohn, via Beethoven.

Kreisler radiated such love, tenderness and compassion that it was easy for me to dream that at one of his concerts at the vast Civic Auditorium in San Francisco he would call me to the stage and give me his glorious Guarnerius del Gusù!

I came to know him quite well upon other occasions in London, Paris and New York and was drawn even closer to him when I realised how similar had been his formation to that of my beloved and great teacher Georges Enesco who had also studied in Vienna with Helmesberger and in Paris with Massart, and that their Vienna-Paris axis, not to speak of our London-New York one, was something I shared intimately with those revered "elders".

We also shared our devotion to English music and our love of our English public. It was to him formally and to me informally that Sir Edward Elgar dedicated his beautiful violin concerto.

Fritz Kreisler's playing was unique and markedly characteristic. His tone, production, incision, lilt, phrasing, rhythmic inflection and accentuation belonged to a born violinist (of which central Europe may boast of a thousand varieties — from improvised gypsy to classical native — a vast region ripe with unparalleled musical germination). His music was always vivacious, provocative and unfailingly fascinating.

It is no wonder he could pick up a violin, after having dropped it for years of medical studies and army service, and resume playing within only eight weeks. No wonder that he always counselled me never to practise! It is because Kreisler never really had to practise that he found the time to bequeath us all the wonderful, so joyful and satisfying works included in this volume.

I was closely connected with the famous "revelation" — for it was in preparation for a concert I was giving in Brooklyn in 1935, one of a series introduced by the distinguished New York music critic Olin Downes, which I opened with the famous Pugnani-Kreisler *Praeludium and Allegro* that Olin Downes could find no documentation for his comments — and finally revealed that benign and magnificent hoax!

Since then that work has opened many hundreds of programmes I gave for American, British and Allied troops during the war of 1939-1945. Many are the works included in this well-edited compilation by Eric Wen which gave such unforgettable pleasure to our audiences of every kind the world over, and which now, thanks to Carl Fischer's edition, will continue to delight humankind as long as it cultivates its voice, its violin and its faltering humanity.

YEHUDI MENUHIN
February 1990

Fritz Kreisler (*circa* 1930)

Fritz Kreisler, 1875-1962

Fritz Kreisler was one of the most popular musical figures of the 20th century. As well known during his career as Caruso and Paderewski, he was acknowledged as the "King of Violinists" and beloved by concert audiences everywhere. Kreisler's playing style was unmistakable. His tone was an extraordinary mixture of tenderness and intensity, and the incisiveness of his bowing infused every note that he played with a rhythmic life of its own.

Born in Vienna on February 2, 1875, Kreisler began learning the violin at the age of four. When he was seven he was admitted to the Vienna Conservatory as the youngest violinist ever to be accepted. He became a pupil of Joseph Helmesberger Jr. and, three years later, won the conservatory's gold medal. Kreisler continued his studies at the Paris Conservatory under Lambert Massart (the teacher of Wieniawski) and at the age of twelve was awarded the conservatory's *premier prix*. After this point Kreisler received no further

formal instruction on the violin. In 1888 the young violinist was heard by the famed pianist Moriz Rosenthal and was engaged as a co-artist for an extended six-month tour in the U.S. Upon his return to Vienna the following year, Kreisler completed his academic studies, attended medical school for two years and served in the Austrian army. Although he laid aside the violin throughout this period, at the age of 21 Kreisler decided to return to music as a profession.

After spending "eight weeks in seclusion and solitude, getting back into my stride and recovering my manual dexterity," Kreisler was ready to make a career as a violinist yet again. Despite several early setbacks (he failed to secure a position in the violin section of the Vienna Court Opera Orchestra), Kreisler eventually achieved his long-deserved recognition as a violin soloist. After touring Scandinavia, Russia and Turkey, he made his début with the Vienna Philharmonic Orchestra under Hans Richter in 1898 and the following year he performed with the Berlin Philharmonic Orchestra under Artur Nikisch. The success of these appearances firmly established Kreisler's reputation, and he went on to become the most important violinist of his time. During World War II Kreisler became an American citizen and settled in New York. He made his last public appearance at Carnegie Hall in 1947, and died on January 29, 1962, a few days before his 87th birthday.

In addition to his achievement as a violinist, Kreisler was an exceptionally gifted composer. He was thoroughly trained in the art of composition and, along with his violin studies at the Vienna and Paris Conservatories, studied harmony and counterpoint with Bruckner and Delibes. Today Kreisler can be regarded as the last exponent of a great tradition of violinist-composers. Beginning in the Italian Baroque with Corelli, Vivaldi and Tartini, this line continued with such 19th-century figures as Kreutzer, Spohr, Paganini, Ernst, Vieuxtemps, Wieniawski and Sarasate. As with the works of his predecessors, Kreisler's many original compositions and transcriptions have now become firmly established as an essential part of the violin repertoire.

Original Compositions

Kreisler published over 150 compositions and arrangements during his career. Considering the extent of his performing activities, it seems quite remarkable that he found any time to compose at all. One especially notable quality of Kreisler's compositions is his natural gift of melody. Many of his works are characterized by a Viennese lilt and charm, and they all display a keen sense of structure and formal design. As Kreisler was himself an expert pianist, the keyboard writing in his pieces is extremely idiomatic. The composer's harmonic inventiveness is enriched further by a penchant for thick and sonorous chords.

Kreisler was particularly gifted as a composer of the violin miniature. Despite their brevity, his violin pieces contain a rich concentration of musical ideas. Although it is these short violin compositions for which he is now remembered, Kreisler also wrote a number of works for different media. In addition to making piano arrangements of his popular violin pieces, he composed a number of songs, a string quartet and two operettas, *Apple Blossoms* and *Sissy*. At the request of a friend, he even composed two football songs for the University of Wisconsin.

Kreisler's *Caprice Viennois* is perhaps the most famous of all the violinist's compositions. The principal theme is presented as a lovely duet in double stops and its subtle shifts between major and minor evoke the quintessentially Viennese mixture of gaiety and wistfulness. This nostalgic mood is relieved by a sparkling middle section containing rapid scales and ricochet bowings. *Tambourin Chinois*, said by the composer to be inspired by the bustling activity of a Chinese restaurant in San Francisco, is a brilliant display of violinistic fireworks. The trademarks of Eastern music are suggested by the work's use of pentatonic scales and the open intervals of the fourth and fifth, but its central section is unmistakably Viennese in character.

While it is well known that Kreisler wrote a number of short pieces under the names of forgotten composers of the 18th century, his ever-popular *Schön Rosmarin, Liebesleid* and *Liebesfreud* were originally presented as posthumous waltzes by Josef Lanner. Kreisler's famous confession of his authorship of the "Classical Manuscripts" which caused such a stir in 1935 was actually preceded by a similar incident 25 years earlier in Berlin. In response to a concert review by the music critic of the *Berliner Tageblatt*, who censured the violinist for "daring" to program his *Caprice Viennois* alongside the waltzes of Lanner, Kreisler revealed his own authorship of the "Lanner" works in question. *Schön Rosmarin* contains delightful staccato passages and a true Austrian *Ländler* as its middle section. *Liebesleid* contrasts the poignant syncopations of its principal theme in minor with the dotted rhythms of a wistful melody set in major, and the joyous *Liebesfreud* is a miniature rondo.

The principal theme of Kreisler's *Rondino* is based on the opening four measures of the little-known Rondo in G for violin and piano (WoO 41) by Beethoven. Kreisler not only transposes the original key to E-flat, but sets a more leisurely tempo by dividing each 6/8 measure of Beethoven's original into two bars of 3/4. Kreisler provides his own contrasting sections to the principal theme and concludes the work with a brief but charming coda.

Although subtitled "Arabo-Spanish Gypsy song of the 18th Century", *La Gitana* is an original composition by Kreisler. It is full of exotic color and begins with improvisatory cadenza-like flourishes. The main theme is accompanied by Flamenco-like rhythms and leads into a lyrical second section. A short coda which echoes the opening introduction concludes the work. Kreisler's *Recitative and Scherzo* is a composition for unaccompanied violin in the style of one of Ysaÿe's solo violin sonatas. The work begins with a richly chromatic recitative in D minor and concludes with a sprightly scherzo (in the relative key of F major) full of rapid passagework and chords.

Fritz Kreisler as a young man (*circa* 1900)

Compositions "in the style of . . ."

In 1905 a series of previously unknown Baroque compositions for violin and piano was published under the title "Classical Manuscripts". The arranger was Fritz Kreisler and he credited a collection of 53 manuscripts discovered "in an old convent in the South of France" as the source of these works. He went on to explain: "Naturally, this music was not all written for violin. I have arranged some of it for my instrument. I have made minor changes in the melodies, and I have modernized the accompaniments to some extent, but I have tried to retain the spirit of the original compositions." As is well known today, Kreisler himself was the composer of these "Baroque" pieces. They figured prominently in the violinist's concert programs and were accepted as works by their attributed composers for over a quarter of a century.

Kreisler's authorship of the "Classical Manuscripts" was discovered in 1935 by Olin Downes, the chief critic of *The New York Times*. Asked to present a lecture comparing a violin arrangement with its original version, Downes selected one of the items in Kreisler's "Classical Manuscripts" for discussion. After looking in several major music research libraries, Downes failed to discover a single source for the work. He contacted the publisher Carl Fischer directly to inquire about the work's origin and thereby found out its true source. Soon afterwards Downes received a telegram from the violinist, explaining: "The entire series labelled 'Classical Manuscripts' are my original compositions . . . Necessity forced this course upon me thirty years ago when I was desirous of enlarging my programs. I found it impudent and tactless to repeat my name endlessly on the programs."

Although several of the violinist's friends had known all along about the "Classical Manuscripts" (Enesco advised the young Menuhin to learn all of Kreisler's work, "irrespective of the strange names connected with them"), Kreisler's "confession" caused a major stir among the musicologists of his day. Ernest Newman, head music critic of *The Times* in London, was particularly incensed and chastised the violinist publically. No doubt embarrassed by his acceptance of the "Classical Manuscripts" as original, Newman belittled the works ("There is nothing whatever in Kreisler's achievement") and claimed that "a vast amount of 17th- and 18th-century music was merely the exploitation of formulae, the effective handling of which is within the scope of any ordinarily intelligent musician today." This denouncement initiated an exchange of letters in *The Times* between the violinist and critic. After reading Newman's article, Kreisler replied: "There was really no necessity for Mr. Newman to worry, for the prestige of a critic with a sense of musical values is not in the least endangered because a piece, which he pronounced good, is found to have been written by another person than he thought. The name changes, the value remains."

Compositions "in the style of . . ."

In response, Newman denied any familiarity with the compositions and reiterated his contention that "any admirably good musician, no matter how modest his endowment for original composition may be, can turn out with perfect ease a manufactured modern article so like the ancient thing it purports to be that listeners everywhere will unquestionably accept it as genuine." In a second reply Kreisler suggested that the critic "be taken at his word and compelled to prove his simple-formula theory, by turning out *in clausura* a specified piece in antique style." This challenge was never taken up by Newman and thus the matter ended in the violinist's favor. Kreisler later referred to the whole affair as a "tempest in a teapot" and posterity has sided with him. The violinist's "Classical Manuscripts" have retained their popularity and continue to appear on concert programs.

Despite the revelation of Kreisler's authorship of the "Classical Manuscripts" over half a century ago, the names of the attributed Baroque composers have been retained in the descriptive phrase "in the style of . . ." following each title. *Praeludium and Allegro* "in the style of Pugnani" is perhaps the most well known of Kreisler's pastiche compositions and was, in fact, the work which led to Olin Downes's discovery. The Praeludium consists of broad arpeggios in the violin accompanied by rich piano chords, and the Allegro contains a variety of violinistic passagework interspersed between statements of the concise main theme.

Kreisler's *Chanson Louis XIII and Pavane* "in the style of Couperin" is colored with a modal quality throughout. According to the

Fritz Kreisler at the age of twelve (*circa* 1887)

composer, the first eight measures of the Chanson are "taken from a traditional melody", and the Pavane which follows is a leisurely dance containing a central section with punchy dotted rhythms. The *Siciliene and Rigaudon*, attributed to the 18th-century French composer François Francoeur, is in the form of two movements from a standard four-movement Baroque sonata. (In Kreisler's day it was common practice to program only one or two movements from a longer work.) The wistful mood of the lovely opening Sicilienne is contrasted by a sprightly Rigaudon in rapid 16th notes.

Finally, Kreisler's *Variations on a theme of Corelli* is based on the Gavotte from Corelli's Sonata No. 10 of Op. 5. The variations are modelled after the 50 in Tartini's *Art of Bowing* and although Kreisler's first variation is similar to one of Tartini's, the second and third variations are completely original. Kreisler modifies Corelli's original theme slightly and provides an elaborate piano accompaniment.

Fritz Kreisler (*circa* 1925)

Transcriptions

Kreisler's transcriptions are notable for their imaginative use of the violin. His knowledge of the instrument's expressive possibilities is clearly reflected in his use of a variety of bowing strokes, harmonics, pizzicato effects and especially double stops. Although he explores these to their fullest they are never employed for virtuoso display alone. Kreisler's writing for the violin always serves to illuminate the musical ideas of the work transcribed.

Mozart's "Haffner" Serenade was composed in 1776 when the composer was 20 years old. Three of its eight movements contain a solo violin part and the Rondo movement has been made especially popular through Kreisler's effective transcription for violin and piano. Although the arrangement remains faithful to the original, Kreisler omits a brief section in C major and transposes the register of the solo part down an octave for several measures in the recapitulation. He also adds three cadenzas, the last of which includes a touching statement in double stops of the Rondo's second theme.

Gluck's opera *Orfeo ed Euridice*, first performed in Paris in 1762, is acknowledged as one of the composer's masterpieces. Kreisler's *Melodie* is a transcription of the opera's instrumental interlude entitled "Dance of the Blessed Spirits." Originally cast for solo flute, the restrained tragic quality of this haunting melody is extremely well suited to the expressive possibilities of the violin. Mendelssohn's *Songs Without Words* were written for solo piano and remain among the composer's best-loved works. The selection included here, originally in G major, is often known by its nickname "May Breezes". Kreisler not only transposes the piece to B-flat, but sets the melody entirely on the G-string of the violin. In addition, he adds a lovely introduction and enriches the accompanying harmony in several places.

Dvořák's *Slavonic Dances* were originally composed for piano four-hands, and later orchestrated by the composer. Kreisler's imaginative setting of the Slavonic Dance in E minor (No. 2 from Op. 72) creates orchestral colors of its own through the use of elaborate double stops, harmonics and ricochet bowings.

Granados' *Spanish Dance* in E minor, originally composed for solo piano, was written when the composer was in his mid-20s, and part of a collection much admired by Massenet, Saint-Saëns and Grieg. Although Kreisler's setting is essentially a straightforward transcription of Granados' original, he provides an original countermelody for the violin in the central middle section. Albeniz's *Tango* is one of six piano pieces entitled "Albumleaves" (Op. 165). In Kreisler's arrangement the piano articulates the deliberate tango rhythm while the violin states the well-known melody in double stops. The *Danse espagnole* by de Falla is from the opera *La Vida Breve*, the work which established the composer's reputation outside Spain. Kreisler's brilliant transcription simulates the sound of castanets and guitars through the effective use of ricochet bowings and pizzicato chords.

Cadenzas

Kreisler's cadenzas are among the most imaginative ever conceived for the violin. Not only do they integrate a composition's many musical ideas, but they fully explore the resources of the instrument. Especially noteworthy in Kreisler's cadenzas is their harmonic interest. Double stops and chords are frequently employed, and quotations of important thematic material are often accompanied by left-hand tremolos on an adjacent string.

Kreisler's cadenza to the first movement of Beethoven's Violin Concerto is justly renowned,

and the passage which combines two of the movement's principal themes is a breathtaking example of the violinist's contrapuntal imagination. Kreisler's cadenzas to the Brahms and Paganini concertos are also extremely attractive. They contain particularly inspired settings of each work's "second" theme in which the melody is stated on one string (the E-string in the Brahms, and the G-string in the Paganini) while being accompanied in full harmony on the other three.

About Eric Wen

Eric Wen was born in New York City in 1953. He attended Columbia and Yale Universities, and was awarded a research grant for advanced study at Cambridge University in England.

As a professional violinist Mr. Wen was a founding member of *L'ensemble Arpeggione*, a chamber group based in France, from 1981-1983. He taught music theory and analysis at

the Mannes College of Music in New York City and the Guildhall School of Music in London, as well as Goldsmith's College at the University of London. He has also published a number of articles in the field of Schenkerian analysis.

Eric Wen was Editor of *The Strad* from 1986-1989, and is currently Editor of *The Musical Times*.

Caprice Viennois

FRITZ KREISLER, Op. 2

4

Tambourin Chinois

FRITZ KREISLER, Op. 3

10

Liebesfreud

FRITZ KREISLER

20

ATF115

Liebesleid

FRITZ KREISLER

Schön Rosmarin

FRITZ KREISLER

meno mosso

28

To Mischa Elman

Rondino
on a theme of Beethoven

FRITZ KREISLER

La Gitana

FRITZ KREISLER

Allegro moderato, quasi Recitativo

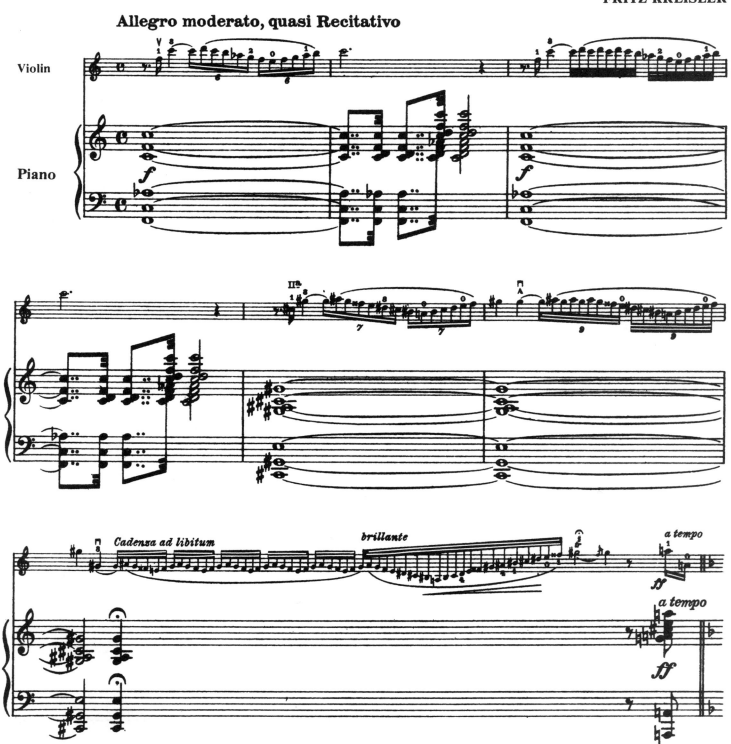

Allegro giusto e ritmico

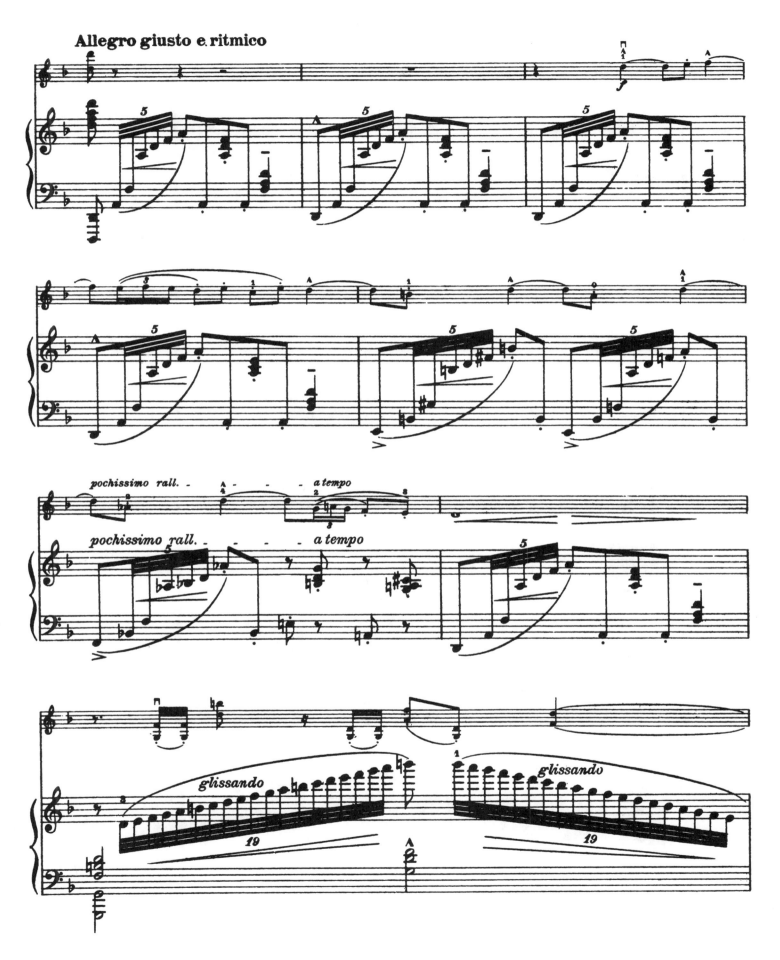

Allegretto grazioso

Variations on a theme by Corelli
In the style of Tartini*

FRITZ KREISLER

*Giuseppe Tartini (1692-1770).

ATF115

44

Var. III
l'istesso tempo

Chanson Louis XIII and Pavane

In the style of Couperin*

Chanson Louis XIII

FRITZ KREISLER

*Louis Couperin (ca. 1626-1661).

attacca

ATF115

48

Pavane

Sicilienne and Rigaudon

In the style of Francoeur*

Sicilienne

FRITZ KREISLER

*François Francoeur (1698-1787).

Rigaudon

Praeludium and Allegro
In the style of Pugnani*

Praeludium

FRITZ KREISLER

*Gaetano Pugnani (1731-1798).

ATF115

Allegro

Allegro molto moderato

62

ATF115

Melodie
from *Orfeo ed Euridice*

CHRISTOPH WILLIBALD von GLUCK
(1714-1787)
Transcribed by Fritz Kreisler

Rondo
from *Serenade in D Major* ("Haffner")

WOLFGANG AMADEUS MOZART, K. 250
(1756-1791)
Transcribed by Fritz Kreisler

74

Song without Words

FELIX MENDELSSOHN, Op. 62, No. 1
(1809-1847)
Transcribed by Fritz Kreisler

ATF115

80

ATF115

Slavonic Dance
in E Minor

ANTONIN DVOŘÁK, Op. 46, No. 2
(1841-1904)
Transcribed by Fritz Kreisler

Andante grazioso quasi Allegretto

Spanish Dance
in E Minor

ENRIQUE GRANADOS
(1867-1916)
Transcribed by Fritz Kreisler

Andantino quasi Allegretto

93

ATF115

Tango

ISAAC ALBENIZ, Op. 165, No. 2
(1860-1909)
Transcribed by Fritz Kreisler

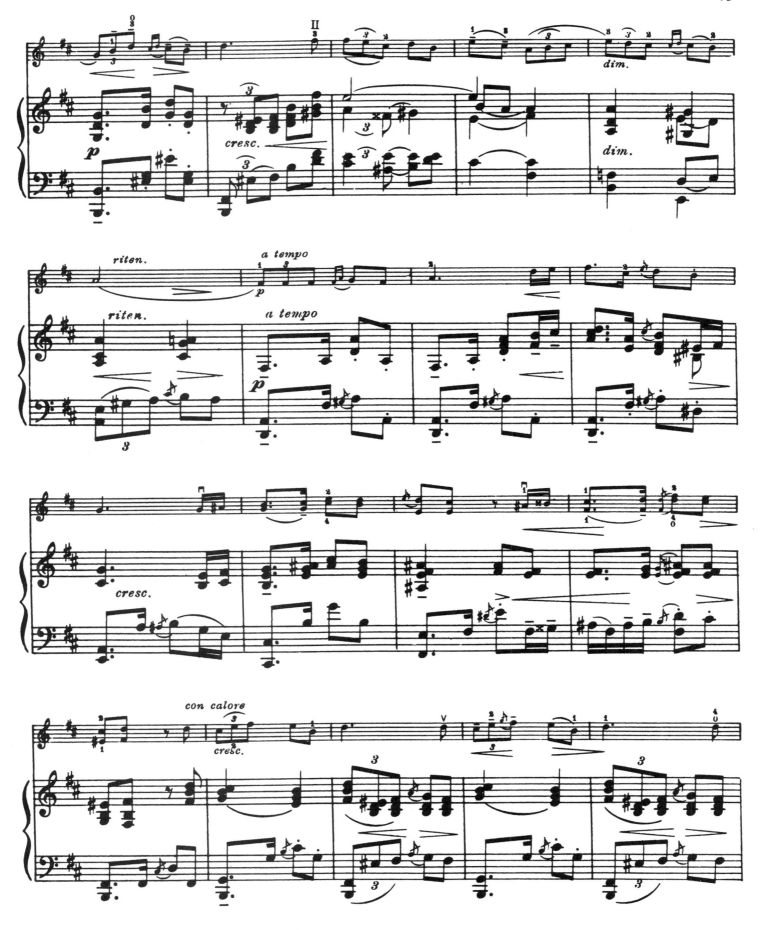

Danse Espagnole

from *La Vida Breve*

MANUEL de FALLA
(1876-1946)
Transcribed by Fritz Kreisler

108

ATF115

Jascha Heifetz
Folios

"The Heifetz Collection" for Violin & Piano
A collection of twenty-four classic Heifetz transcriptions along with a bonus of two violin concerto cadenzas that are part of the legacy and legend of the "father of modern, virtuoso violin playing." This edition contains separate piano and violin parts, that are expertly edited, engraved and printed to provide many years of use and pleasure. Foreword by Itzhak Perlman.
(Cat. No. ATF116)

"New Favorite Encore Folio" for Violin & Piano
This fine collection of fifteen compositions was selected and edited by Heifetz and presented in outstanding engravings and printing. Compositions include "Rigaudon", "Zapateado," "Guitarre" in addition to pieces by Schubert, Mendelssohn, Mozart, Brahms and Schumann among others.
(Cat. No. O2137)